You Have Got to Be Good at Something

Failing Grades Don't Equal Failing at Life

Book One of the Series
Under His True Light
Biblical Survival Guides for Everyday Preteens

Zanna Noe

You Have Got to Be Good at Something
Failing Grades Don't Equal Failing at Life
By Zanna Noe

Copyright © 2017 by Zanna Noe
All rights reserved.

No part of this publication may be reproduced, stored in a retrieval system, or transmitted (electronic, mechanical, photocopy, recording, or any other way) without the written permission of the copyright holder, except as permitted by U.S. copyright law.

Scripture quotations are taken from the Holy Bible, New Living Translation, copyright ©1996, 2004, 2007, 2013, 2015 by Tyndale House Foundation. Used by permission of Tyndale House Publishers, Inc., Carol Stream, Illinois 60188. All rights reserved.

Illustrated in part by Amy Stokes

For every preteen who
believes in God and seeks Him daily

Jacob, 12

We had a test in Social studies today, and I failed again. That stinks!

I don't know why they have to give those tests on Thursdays and Fridays.

I think teachers do it on purpose so they can bomb kids' weekends.

Dad will probably eat me alive and won't let me play video games. Worse than that, they might pull me out of my hockey team. That's bad! I just now learned how to be awesome at right wing.

My mom will be upset again. Since she lost her job, she thinks my bad grades are making things even worse.

I don't know who came up with the idea of grades anyway. I'd hate my job if I was a teacher.

School Isn't Always Cool

Would you like your school much better if you had good grades only?

You may think that straight "A" students make teachers' work and parents' lives easier. Otherwise, they would never make those "proud parent of an honor roll student" bumper stickers.

What if a family doesn't have any honor roll students in their household? Do they feel like they are missing something?

Getting a bad grade isn't fun, and it can easily cut your confidence in half. Any failure is draining, especially when you try hard to do your best.

Let's say:

You do your homework,

Participate in the class,

Ask your parents for help

And it still doesn't show much on your report card.

Then you look at some of the students in your class who hardly ever pay any attention to a teacher and are careless about their homework (or they make it look that way) but they still pass their test and get a good grade every time. It is not fair!

I pray that God, the source of hope, will fill you completely with joy and peace because you trust in him. Then you will overflow with confident hope through the power of the Holy Spirit. — Romans 15:13

Isabella, 11

I told myself not to cry, but I can't help it every time I see my mom crying. She was so excited about taking Gabe to that school her friends raved about. Little did she know that they would run an admission test on Gabe, and he isn't even six!

After we filled out a giant stack of forms, a short lady with big glasses and long gray hair took him away from us. For two straight hours!

I was kind of worried, but we were told that she was some kind of specialist and she has tested kids at their school for a hundred years or something like that.

They didn't talk to Gabe or me too much after that test but they invited Mom for a private talk.

She was so upset after that meeting she could barely drive. I'm glad we didn't crash.

They told her that our Gabe was delayed! Gabe? Delayed?! I'm not sure about their tests, but I really think Gabe is pretty smart.

Do they know that he started riding his bike without training wheels when he was four? He can sing perfectly any tune he hears from TV or on my MP3 player. My little brother finds all the websites and apps better than I do!

One time some older kids took my scooter away and I didn't even know it. Gabe tracked them down and fought it out for me. He's a very cool kid.

You Have Got To Be Good At Something

Did you know that every person on Earth, adult or child, has a unique, God- given talent for at least one thing?

Being academically successful is one of the talents that belong to some people. That's why completing an assignment or passing a test comes as easily as a piece of cake to them. Meanwhile, most kids usually work hard in order to bring their grades up.

Sometimes going to bed on time and eating healthy food make your schoolwork easier, but stress and fear of failing can hold you tight and idle like a broken down chain on your bike.

Don't get discouraged or disappointed if you don't belong to the group of the best students in your class. Instead, think of something you are really good at. The way you know it is:

- You almost always enjoy the activity.
- It comes fairly easy to you.
- You get a lot of compliments and thanks for your work.

Even if you are good at shopping or video games, you can contribute and be creative. For example, you might help your family by comparing the prices to save money or you and your friends/siblings can try to create a new video game.

If you are confident about your special talent, look for an opportunity to use it as much as you can.

Help Needed

Have you ever read in the Old Testament about men who built a new place of worship from scratch?

The LORD has filled Bezalel with the Spirit of God, giving him great wisdom, ability, and expertise in all kinds of crafts. He is a master craftsman, expert in working with gold, silver, and bronze. He is skilled in engraving and mounting gemstones and in carving wood. — Exodus 35:31–33

Did you know that the skills they're talking about are very important and valuable today?

- Many churches, schools, building companies and designers are always looking for skillful people.
- If you have talent for any craft, keep your eyes or your ears open for the projects that can use your skills.
- You might have to start simple by helping your family and friends or by volunteering at your school with building and decorating needs.

EMILY, 10 and JULIE, 11

JULIE: You are not listening to what I'm saying, Emily. Are you okay?

EMILY: Yes, I'm just thinking about something else.

JULIE: Like what?

EMILY: My mom wants me to restart my piano lessons again.

JULIE: I didn't know you quit.

EMILY: I didn't officially quit but I stopped practicing. So, my mom stopped paying for the lessons.

JULIE: What about your teacher?

EMILY: She called us and she told me not to quit.

JULIE: I think she's right. Everybody likes your songs. Are you still, what's that word… composing?

EMILY: That's the thing. My grades aren't that great. Dad thinks I should spend more time on my homework.

JULIE: Oh brother!

EMILY: Speaking about my brother, he thinks my songs are too annoying. Our piano is in the living room.

JULIE: Is there any way you can move it?

EMILY: I don't know. I'll ask Dad.

JULIE: Don't give up, write some more songs. I'll help you to put them on YouTube.

EMILY: Thank you.

Sing To The Joy!

Chenaniah, chief of the Levites, was in charge of the singing; he gave instruction in singing because he was skillful. — 1 Chronicles 15:22

Most preschool children like to sing. They enjoy music without any doubts because they aren't afraid to be imperfect. Younger boys and girls typically aren't shy to be loud or sing out of tune.

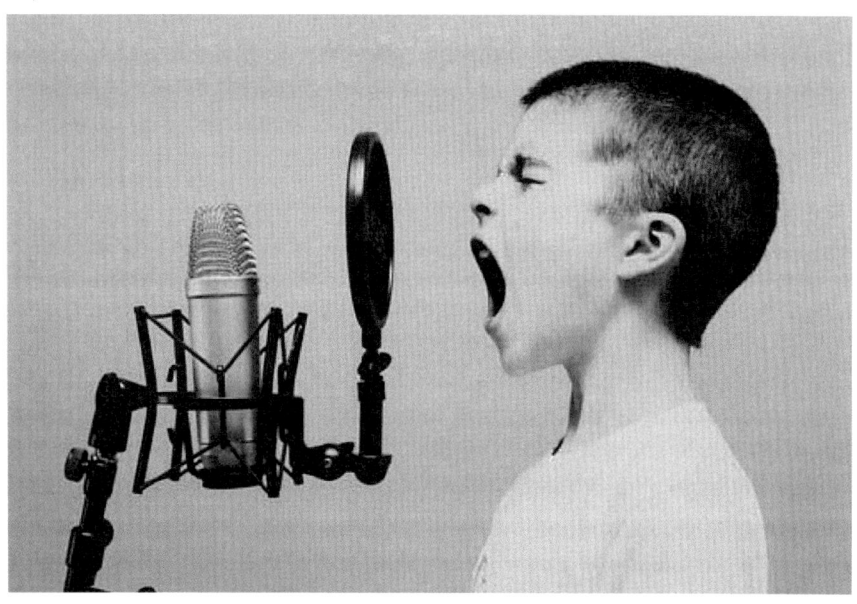

Why do you think we have to make music anyway when we can download any music we want today?

Also, many times when you aren't little anymore and you sing or play an instrument, your parent or sibling might ask you to stop because they find your practice annoying.

Yet, strangely enough, most people today aren't annoyed with yelling and bad words they hear on screen.

Try to make music anyway because if you don't, you will never find out how good or how bad you are at it.

- You know by now that it takes some discipline and solid practice to get good results in making music.
- Practice with the headphones on or when you are by yourself.
- Record yourself if you can.
- Many schools have a band, an orchestra or a choir and many churches need young musicians. If your school doesn't have a music program, check to see if your town has community music ensembles you can join.

Tell the Story

God gave these four young men an unusual aptitude for understanding every aspect of literature and wisdom. — Daniel 1:17

You may not get a high score on your reading and writing test, but you may enjoy reading books or drawing cartoons.

- If you can understand and retell the story to make it clear and entertaining for others, you have a talent.

Got Some Logic?

This man Daniel, whom the king named Belteshazzar, has exceptional ability and is filled with divine knowledge and understanding. He can interpret dreams, explain riddles, and solve difficult problems. — Daniel 5:12

Not too many schools will teach you how to interpret your dreams. However, some people have a natural gift called logic.

- Are you good at riddles, puzzles or playing chess?
- Solving difficult problems is a very important skill required for professions like managers, lawyers, politicians and computer programmers.

PATRICIA, 10

My Aunt Stephaney is staying with us for this Spring break. I like her a lot, she's always stylish and smells good.

Aunt Stephaney gives me a lot of attention, since she doesn't have her own children.

We go to all kinds of museums and concerts. It's really fun!

Thank goodness she doesn't ask me about my grades at school. She just questioned me about my interest in the arts and I didn't really know what to tell her.

I participated in a puppet show last year, but I didn't enjoy it that much. Maybe because I only had one line. The rest of it was just waiting in line on stage in total darkness.

Then my aunt asked me about sports and she told me all about her high school basketball memories. It seemed like she really had a good time. I tried soccer one season and I pretty much stunk to be honest. The tough girls who were really good at it didn't like me much.

I didn't tell her anything about my volunteering job at the hospital where I go on Wednesdays and read to the sick kids. I just didn't feel like bragging about it.

God Works in Different Ways

Let's say you don't really have any skills mentioned above.

Just know and be confident that you are perfectly normal.

Has anybody ever told you about spiritual gifts? You may not realize it but you have a spiritual gift, probably more than one and it outweighs all of the honor rolls, trophies or diplomas you can possibly think of.

God works in different ways, but it is the same God who does the work in all of us. — 1 Corinthians 12:6

A spiritual gift is given to each of us so we can help each other. — 1 Corinthians 12:7

Wise Advice

Unless you are a loner who lives away from everybody else, you are surrounded by people at least a few hours a day. Therefore, you always have a chance to use your spiritual gift by simply helping someone next to you.

To one person the Spirit gives the ability to give wise advice; to another the same Spirit gives a message of special knowledge. — 1 Corinthians 12:8

Have you heard about bad and good choices you can make every day? Well, some kids can't tell the difference between good and bad.

- We don't know why but those two terms got confused at some point in their lives. They need someone who can give them a right direction and advice.

- Do you have a special gift of guiding others? If you go to school, do sports or go to an enrichment program, there is always an opportunity to use it.

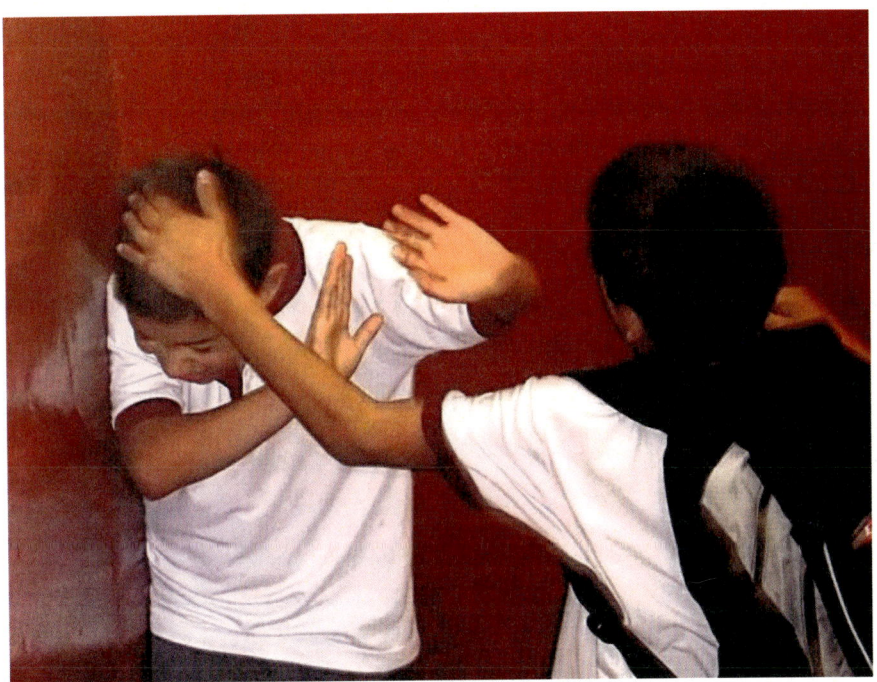

Nothing to Show Off

If you are a dancer or an athlete, you probably get plenty of trophies to show for your efforts and time spent.

Have you ever got any rewards or grades for just being kind?

JUSTIN, 11

Coach Roger yelled at Tracy again, because he doesn't tackle as good as he used to.

I've known Trace for a long time now. He's a really nice guy. His knee got messed up somehow and he is in lots of pain every time we practice or play the game. He never says anything about it though.

I found out about it from my mom because she knows his mom. Trace doesn't want to go to therapy and he keeps saying he's all right. He isn't though, but he wants to look tough. Football is his favorite sport, I bet.

I'm not going to tell anybody about his knee, I don't think he wants me to. But I don't want other dudes to hurt him even more. I don't want Coach Roger to kick him off of our team either. So, I'll see if I can talk Trace into going to his therapy sessions.

If your gift is serving others, serve them well. If you are a teacher, teach well. If your gift is to encourage others, be encouraging. If it is giving, give generously. If God has given you leadership ability, take the responsibility seriously. And if you have a gift for showing kindness to others, do it gladly. — Romans 12:7–8

MARCUS, 9

Mom is talking on the phone. Sounds, like she's inviting the Martins over. I don't know what to do. I like Ryan a lot, but I'm not sure about his mom.

All she likes to talk about is tests and grades. They must be really bothering her. I feel bad for Ryan. Does his mom want to be a teacher or something?

I feel bad for myself too. I wish my mom had something to brag about. My grades aren't all that good. Actually, they are okay, but below good, whatever…Maybe, I can sneak out of the house, before they come…

Why Do I Need Grades Anyway?

Why do we need to be graded at school anyway? Most kids who have bad luck with their grades wish to eliminate them fast, like unwanted files on their computer screens.

- Grading students is part of your teacher's job. A lot of home schooling parents have to grade their own kids. Yikes!
- Every job or study requires some kind of evaluation. Most schools use grading system to evaluate their students.
- If your parents are working, they go through evaluations too. In the adult world they call it a "review." When you work for somebody else, you get a review from your boss or a supervisor.
- Business owners get reviews from their customers, so they know how good or how bad their services and products are.
- Musicians, actors and other artists get reviews from the critics, who can describe how well or how poorly they performed.

- Schools and teachers are evaluated by the board of education and get scores. They can also get a good or bad reputation from students' parents. That's how they get evaluated by all the families living in that district.

We don't know why but God evaluated Himself as soon as He created the Earth.

Then God looked over all he had made, and he saw that it was very good! — Genesis 1:31

You Are Not Alone

Adults usually feel frustrated and sad after getting a bad review, the same way as their kids feel when they get a bad grade.

- Don't be afraid of your mom's or dad's reaction to your failure.
- No matter how disappointed they look or act that day, they still love you just as much as you love them regardless of their professional failures or poor relationships at work.

JOSHUA, 9 and ZACH, 10

ZACH: I'm glad it's Friday. Are you coming over today?

JOSHUA: I don't know. I still have homework to do.

ZACH: Really? I don't want to waste my weekends on homework, it's not worth it.

JOSHUA: What do you mean?

ZACH: Well, I did all my work the whole last semester and I got lame report card anyway. What's the point in sweating over my homework?

JOSHUA: Did your mom and dad get mad at you?

ZACH: They weren't mad, they were disappointed. Dad even thinks I have mean teachers.

JOSHUA: Nah, everybody's got the same teachers.

ZACH: Do you think that the person with bad grades is stupid or something?

JOSHUA: No, I don't think that at all. You are smart and funny. I like to hang out with you.

Think of a Good Friend

- Think of a good friend you have known for a while who often enjoys your company and embraces your friendship with all of your personality qualities as well as downfalls.
- A good friend doesn't normally care much about your report cards or trophies. Share your concerns with that boy or girl.
- Be honest about your grades and your evaluation you received at school, it can be very enjoyable to complain or laugh about it as much as you want to.
- Pray together

We also pray that you will be strengthened with all his glorious power so you will have all the endurance and patience you need. May you be filled with joy, always thanking the Father — Colossians 1:11–12

Be Honest with Yourself

Did you actually try everything to bring your grades up or did you just stop somewhere halfway? Our best intention for cleaning our room often turns into finding new excuses so we can wait until next week.

Are there too many after school activities in the way of your homework? Maybe one enrichment program or a ministry is good enough if your school feels like a struggle.

SONYA, 12

I have to finish my homework on the bus. I wasted all my free time studying for my test yesterday.

I don't think I can pass it, I will fail again. I'm hungry, but if I eat breakfast, I'll throw up at school like I did last time.

Mom said that if I have one bad grade, she won't pay for my dance lessons.

My teachers have no idea that I stay up til one a.m. so I can get ready for the test. I'm so tired, I wish I could fast forward this day, can't wait until the weekends.

Another Extreme

Many kids spend huge amounts of time on homework and still think it's not enough to get it done. Are you one of them? Do you have a friend with this issue? If so, you are probably having too many distractions either at home or on your mind, which makes it almost impossible to focus.

- Set a predictable time after school and stick to that schedule
- Eliminate video games, phone and TV.
- Find a quiet place away from barking dogs, ringing telephones, media sets or noisy brothers and sisters.

(Although, if you are raised in a big family, some background noises will always be there and you are probably used to them by now.)

- If your school or a particular class seems to be too difficult, it probably is. Do not be afraid to address the struggle to your parents and teachers. High expectations and academic pride are motivating for some kids, but some families find them quite stressful and destructive.
- You don't have to focus on somebody else's achievements, trying to keep up; focus on God and His will instead.

We ask God to give you complete knowledge of his will and to give you spiritual wisdom and understanding. Then the way you live will always honor and please the Lord, and your lives will produce every kind of good fruit. All the while, you will grow as you learn to know God better and better. — 2 Corinthians 4:17-18

Help is Always Available

Like in everything else, help is always available to you and it's closer than you think.

- Many communities offer free help with homework in person or over the phone. Ask about it at your local library.
- There are also free tutors who can be found either on the internet or at one of your local schools.

- You and your friends can share your gifts with each other. One of you might be stronger at math and another can help with the composition writing. Your own homework club can be fun and productive as long as you are staying away from distractions.
- Share your faith with your friends.

Then he saw wisdom and evaluated it.

He set it in place and examined it thoroughly.

And this is what he says to all humanity:

'The fear of the Lord is true wisdom;

to forsake evil is real understanding.'

– Job 28: 27-28

Zanna Noe, M.Ed is a teacher, writer, musician and a mother of three sons. She created the *Under His True Light* series to help everyday preteens to navigate common and unique struggles in their lives without losing hope, courage and strong faith. The family resides in Dallas, TX.

You can follow her on Facebook and Instagram.

For questions and comments write to undertruelight@gmail.com

Made in the USA
San Bernardino, CA
07 July 2017